What Happens When Your Heart Breaks?

Erin M. Arnold

LOST BLONDE

A Lost Blonde Original Paperback

The following poems have been previously published:

Lips: SHINE Poetry Series

Comforter Pantoum: SHINE Poetry Series

Stop Breaking My Heart and I'll Stop Seeking Reparations: SHINE Poetry Series & SHINE Quarterly, Issue 2

ISBN 979-8-9924345-8-3

10 9 8 7 6 5 4 3 2 1

Published by Lost Blonde Literary

www.lostblondelit.com

Cheers to the heartbreakers. Also, how dare you?

Contents

Lips

Trust me when I say this word
is right on the tip of my lips.

I get so distracted with
your fingertips on my lips.

Stuttering, sputtering, four letters
playing such a trick on my lips.

Cyan eyes spilling secrets
unwilling to slip from my lips.

Pulse pounding on my sleeve. Trust
me, love on the tip of my lips.

Ever reticent in nightly
omission—the sin of my lips.

Marie Antoinette

like the last queen of France, you've got me losing my head
you keep feeding me cake when I'm looking for bread
everything's so sugary sweet when you lay me in bed
at the end of this all we'll both wind up dead

like Romeo and Juliet, killed by misunderstanding
like Icarus, who had too much faith in his wax wings
like Greek heroes, lulled into rocks by sweet nothings
our love exists among art and life's greatest tragedies

Honeycrisp

apple-body girl
round in all the wrong places
no make-up to make up for my average
face but my upper lip has you planning
houses with white fence pickets—rub me
the right way and I'll grant all your wishes
wildest dreams have nothing on me
and my honeycrisp delicious
apple body

Chance

Brilliant mind,
mismatched eyes.
I never stood a chance.

Lovely words,
moved heaven and earth.
I never stood a chance.

Fell faster
than it could last, dear.
We never stood a chance.

Love & Wonder

What does it mean to love the
life you lead? To love the person you
see in the mirror? To breathe without
uncertainty of self and the man
who lies beside you? Who lives within you.
Who whispers truths like violets are blue
and promises every hue in the
gloaming to you? Who delivers tears
rarely, orgasms nightly, and blonde
soy vanilla lattes on demand.
Instagram official. Easy. Surely it is
not unpleasant. Not shouting in the
basement hoping the kids don't hear us.
Turning our backs to the fear that the
end might be near us. Seeking cheerful
therapists with ivory couches
and towers filled with godless
Gottman success stories.
Love? It cannot be this thing.
So frightening. So abstract.
So unphotographable.

There are no hardware stores open past midnight in the village

so if you need a hammer at 1:00 a.m.
you're shit out of luck

when every solution is a nail
every problem is two pieces
of pine that need to come together

flush corners, although slightly
off center—level with me:
hardware excursions aside

what else are you banging
in the wee hours of the morning?

Evening Fragment, after Sappho

Dusk brings butterflies—
lead in my guts.
Entwined in moonbeams
& wrinkled weathered bedsheets.

Contented in dreamless sleep—
midnight rises.
Skin on skin
& excited conversation

between lovers
dreading dawn
when sun illuminates
character more clearly.

>*All the while, believe me, I prayed*
>*Our night would last twice as long.*

A List of Things to Look Forward To

You pick her up.
We were always dying as slow as a tree.
You put your fingers in her mouth.
Thinking if there were leaves,
You grab her from behind while she makes
            agonizing new use of your office chair.
there was life. Believing as long as
You dance with her in her favorite dress.
we settled into love, you
You push her against the wall and take her breath
            away with passionate kisses.
wouldn't settle for limerence. When
You bite her earlobes.
the love of your life
You tell her what you want her to do to you.
only lasts eleven years it's clear as night
You run your hands over her while you
            pretend to watch her student films.
that the leaves were falling
You use those hands until she moans in ecstasy.
all along.

Bioluminescence

It rains on the riverbed,
bringing out lights like you never left.

Every drop glistening and listening
to how deep I am underwater in you.

Fifteen Minutes

I knew it was her from your Instagram likes, which gave me her name and within fifteen minutes Google gave me her address, phone number, place of employment, hobbies, and the YouTube channel she posted your sex tape on. It was okay because it was easy. Easy. Fifteen minutes to learn her favorite poet. Her favorite performer. Her wife's name. Fifteen minutes to see the reflection on her television as she watched her shitty films on another YouTube channel with only two followers. Fifteen minutes doesn't make an obsession. Fifteen minutes to see if you were in any of her TikTok's. Fifteen minutes to listen to the Spotify playlist she made for you. Fifteen-minute increments to figure out why she was better for you than I was. She gobbled content and in doing so left her footprints everywhere, but none of them told me if you picked her because she did that thing I would only do once. None of her tweets told me how many times you saw her. Just fifteen more minutes to understand why her. Fifteen more minutes to know why not me.

Lessons

I can teach you all the ways to deceive me
if you promise never to leave me.
I may be a novelty, but baby
you were my life.

I'll swallow whatever you feed me
just tell me to open wide.
I'm starving, darling,
stay by my side.

This reminds me of that time

When he left his phone in the car that I took to the baby's appointment and when the messages kept alerting, I couldn't help but reply, "This is his girlfriend, may I ask to whom I'm speaking?" And later he indignantly showed me the reply where she told him he owed her money for the drugs now that she knew he was a liar too and thought that proved his point.

When we drove to his friend's apartment and that girl was there who kept calling me Roxanne and when he gave her a ride home that took over two hours, I sat up in the dark wondering why I was even invited if not to be reminded that I was the spare.

When I was good enough for Saturday nights, but not Sunday brunches.

When he loved me, but not that way. When he loved me too much, but not himself so the timing wasn't right. When he loved himself too much and I couldn't possibly hold a candle.

All of this reminds me of the time when all of this happened before.

Consumer Warning

I'm nothing special and I remind anyone who dares to think otherwise. Anyone who might mistake any light in my eyes for promise or promises of something great. I'm just a chubby girl from the suburbs who sometimes smells of lilacs and regularly reeks of missed opportunities, anxiety, and awareness of her own mortality. There's no magic in an accidental smile. No glimmer of hope in tearful eyes. Just honesty. And oddity. And wishing I was anyone but me, anywhere but here.

Apologies

I need to hear you say you're sorry
        more than I need to hear you say you love me.
Love doesn't mean anything,
        if you got off on the hurting.
Just tell me that you're sorry.

I'll pretend you can look me in the eyes
        when we listen to *Such Great Heights*,
and I'll ignore you
        running out the door,
the hickeys on your neck,
        and all the lies you spat at me.

Just tell me how sorry you are.
        Tell me you regret it.
Don't say you loved me all along,
        and could hurt me anyway.

When We Drive

Taking you back means
taking a backseat.

Knocking the wind out
to remind me I'm breathing.

Heartache is fleeting—
that wagging tongue has me believing
we could be anything again.

my babe

looking for reasons to stay alive, i find that the soundtrack of
our life has been reduced to a pick-up line. as long as you feel
safe, i'll stand here in the corner. no need to look back to me
when you found her looking forward. she and i have the same
dress and i'll always wonder did you dance with us both? kiss
both of our necks? whisper in our ears? run your hand up our
thighs? did you think of me when you asked her to spend the
night? don't worry, babe, in the end i'll survive it—we never
set out to destroy each other, that's just where the lies led.
you made a bed with her, and i just can't lie in it. you came
back to life with me, but i just can't buy into it.
i only wanted to stay alive, but the soundtrack of our life has
been reduced to a pick-up line.

Villanelle for Persephone

Persephone, she haunts me.
Ripe pomegranates, ever tempting.
Everything I wasn't and could never be.

A mere mortal, I only breathe,
while she heralds in the spring.
Persephone, she haunts me.

Plundering lovers from Aphrodite
without inhibition. She's flaunting
everything I wasn't and could never be.

Abducted, she is what he perceives.
Seduction, never leave him wanting.
Persephone, she haunts me.

One day, back to hell she flees.
(For succubus sunlight can be daunting)
Everything I wasn't and could never be.

I much prefer Hecate,
Goddess of immolating giants and setting boundaries.
Done haunting me, poor Persephone—
everything I wasn't and would never be.

Stop Breaking My Heart and I'll Stop Seeking Reparations

Which is a funny way of saying that I only ever expected the truth from you, and when you couldn't deliver, your righteous indignation left no room for my hard-earned disappointment. Which is a funny way of saying that I only ever asked that you keep your mouth for me, and by that I meant your lips, your tongue, your words of affirmation. Which is a funny way of saying that I would never expect you to make it right, you could only ever make it so wrong, but you did it so beautifully. Which is a funny way of saying I miss you, desperately, and can only take solace in these words, which remind me that we weren't perfect even when my memory seems so inclined to deceive me. Which is a funny way of saying I only need to heal now. Which is a funny way of saying I need to go now. Which is a funny thing to say when I can't gather myself outside of your bed.

she's allowed to exist

of course she is.

all she does is exist.

in my mind,
my nightmares,
in your bed and
fantasies.

in that pitch
black memory
where you sigh in
satisfaction and
she laughs

at how foolish I
am.

Comforter Pantoum

There's a stranger in our bed.
When I couldn't stay, I thought
you would save   my   space
but there's a stranger in our bed.

When I couldn't stay, I thought
I heard you say her name.
Now there's a stranger in our bed
while you drift off to sleep.

I heard you. Say her name,
I sigh—she giggles
while you drift. Off to sleep,
sweet dreams my enemy,

I sigh. She giggles.
There's a stranger in our bed.
Silly me, thinking I could come back.
I thought you would save my   space.

Lullabies

Remember that one time
you held my heart in your hands
and carried it, ever so gently
as though it were your own

whispering sweet nothings,
like lullabies, into each chamber
keeping it beating
while you borrowed it?

Even with a hole in my chest
the thing was safer with you
than it ever was with me.

A treasure above any other,
trusted over my head
or eyes or ears or gut.

I finally got it back
still, lulled by lies
an empty and useless pound of flesh
paid in penance for the sin of loving you.

The end of it all, and nothing (with Jack Kerouac)

The time has come for us
My love. My friend.
So, this is what the end looks like—
grey skies, teary-eyed sunsets.

In this mess we created with only love.
Not trust.
Not compassion.
No companionship left.
Because nothing ever happened – not even this.

We were never in Moraine Valley
Arguing with each other and the end. Never
burn, burn, burning like a fabulous yellow roman candle
in the pristine wide valley
beautiful to behold but wasted on us
so close to the sky and the finish line, finding ourselves
exploding like spiders across the stars

Did we ever stop on the side of the road
to admire the Bixby Creek Bridge and the precipice
of the past and the Pacific Coast Highway?
Looking to the horizon to find something past madness, past
being *mad to live, mad to talk, mad to be saved.*

There were never tears on my arm when your parents died.
Never a rush to change the song when our daughter arrived.
No getting naked in abandoned parking lots.
We never traded novels, traded stories, traded songs, traded
forget-me-nots.

Forget me not,
My love, my friend.
The end of it all and nothing.
We were nothing – not even this.

43

Umbrella

Walking home from a funeral yesterday
I crossed paths with two lovers
gazing into one another's eyes

with a reverberating promise
that would have been magical
had I not just buried you.

Palpable electricity shocked even me
from the other side of the street.

The cutest little rain couldn't bother them.
They meandered down the street to brunch,
or their bed, to fall into each other vigorously.

I pulled out my umbrella, the green one you gave me the last
time I left your apartment.
There had been no point in opening it then,
no possibility of salvation from the torrent.

Today I let it cover me, a day late and dollar short.
Too poor to know the difference in riches
when they aren't written in stone and on linen.

Ghosted

Perhaps it just would be
better to never know you
or to pretend you had me as
anything other than a saved space
me, a placeholder
while you hide from your sins
after all this, being in your orbit
completely erases my glow
and I'd like to give up hopeless-ness
I think I'll run for my life
a feat I've attempted before
this time it'll stick.

Suburbia

I packed up a white picket fence to have something to use to
cage in my dreams.
I birthed babies who might grow up to hate me and the fence
I kept them in.
I had men who didn't deserve me, still I let them think they
were my kings,
And I their concubine to cum on and walk away from
whenever they pleased,
Leaving me to wash myself off and pick up the pieces I
handed out so freely.
I whitewashed that fence so no one could really see me
except through pristine slats.
A visionary in that cage of my own making, slowly learning it
might be more important to be
able
to breathe
instead of suffocating on the notion that dinner had to be on
the table by 5.

How to find your self-worth again after being completely eviscerated

Get eight hours of sleep at night, so you wake up feeling like anything is possible. Make sure you immediately get out of bed in the morning to get in the shower – and afterwards definitely don't sit on the edge of your bed in a towel that needs fabric softener to wonder what could have happened if... Definitely stand naked in front of your gilded mirror and marvel at every rose gold stretch mark and navy varicose vein and definitely don't convince yourself that nobody could ever cum with such a body in their sheets. Definitely wear that dress that highlights your tits or ass or arms or whatever your favorite appendage is and definitely don't put on oversized panties underneath. You should put on a full face of make-up. Or don't. Because fuck 'em. Fuck anyone who says you need it. Fuck anyone who says it's too much.

It's your face, after all.

Humility

In my excellence I
pull myself
apart so you know
I am still in my
rightful place

and when I
burst open and the fluorescent
glow from my guts can
no longer be hidden I

will stitch myself up
with your mediocrity.
Rest easy babe as I
lay awake—bursting at the seams.

What Happens When Your Heart Breaks?

When your heart breaks you spend ten minutes before a meeting fixing your eyeliner so your boss doesn't think you're calling him an asshole because you're emotional. You make your kids dinner and tell them you already ate but the truth is you just can't stomach the thought of them at someone else's table. You write a poem in the dark instead of slicing your skin open so you can crawl out of it. You pay the mortgage when all you want to do it burn down the house that you believed was your home together. When your heart breaks you breathe against your better judgement. You get a new haircut. You get a new outfit. You get a new online dating profile that you won't ever swipe right on. When your heart breaks you exist – you're not living if you're not doing it with a broken heart. You sing songs. You collapse in the shower. You read books on healing. You think you'll never heal. You walk hand in hand with it. When your heart breaks but keeps on beating in spite of itself you resent it. You embrace it. What happens when your heart breaks? You gather all of the sad little pieces together and make a go of it again.

Strangers Again

How did we start as strangers and end as strangers as though
no time existed in-between where you knew the deepest parts
of me, and I you?

No longer friends, our secrets are secrets again.

About the Author

Erin M. Arnold is a poet living in Northern Illinois. She has an MFA in poetry from Lindenwood University and looks forward to regularly getting her heart broken. You can find her online at www.erinmarnoldwrites.com.